Emil Nikolaus von
REZNICEK

DONNA DIANA
OVERTURE
Edited by
Richard W. Sargeant, Jr.

Study Score
Partitur

SERENISSIMA MUSIC, INC.

ORCHESTRA

Piccolo (also 3rd Flute)

2 Flutes

2 Oboes

2 Clarinets (A)

2 Bassoons

4 Horns (F)

2 Trumpets (C)

Timpani

Triangle

Harp

Violin I

Violin II

Viola

Violoncello

Double Bass

Duration: ca. 6 minutes

Premiere: December 16, 1894 (with the opera)
Prague, Neu Deutsches Theater
NDT Orchestra / Rudolf Krzyzanowski

ISMN: 979-0-58042-108-1
This score is a newly-engraved edition based upon the first edition
of the opera full score issued in 1895 by J. Schuberth of Leipzig.

Printed in the USA
First Printing: August, 2018

DONNA DIANA OVERTURE

E.N. von Reznicek
Edited by Richard W. Sargeant, Jr.

42202

4

So rasch und leicht als möglich
(as quickly and lightly as possible)

So rasch und leicht als möglich
(as quickly and lightly as possible)

25
16
1.
Fl.
1
2
3
poco f
p
Ob.
p poco espress.
Cl.
Bn.
Hn.
4
Tpt.
Timp.
Tgl.
Vn.
div. pizz.
unis.
pizz.
Va.
Vc.
Cb.

30
Fl.
1
2
3
f
più f
to picc.
1.
Ob.
f espress.
poco f
Cl.
Bn.
a2
Hn.
Tpt.
Timp.
Tgl.
Vn.
arco
Va.
Vc.
Cb.

49
41
Picc.
Fl. 1 2
Ob. 1 2
Cl. 1 2
Bn. 1 2
Hn. 1 2 3 4
1.
3.
Tpt. 1 2
Timp.
Tgl.
Vn. 1 2
Va.
Vc.
Cb.
unis.
pizz.
arco
p
f

52
to fl.
Picc.
p cresc.
Fl. 1 2
p cresc.
Ob. 1 2
p cresc.
Cl. 1 2
p cresc.
Bn. 1 2
p cresc.
Hn. 1 2
3.
3 4
f dim. sempre
Tpt. 1 2
Timp.
Tgl.
p
52
Vn. 1
pizz.
f
più f
2
pizz.
f
più f
Va.
pizz.
f
più f
Vc.
pizz.
f
più f
Cb.

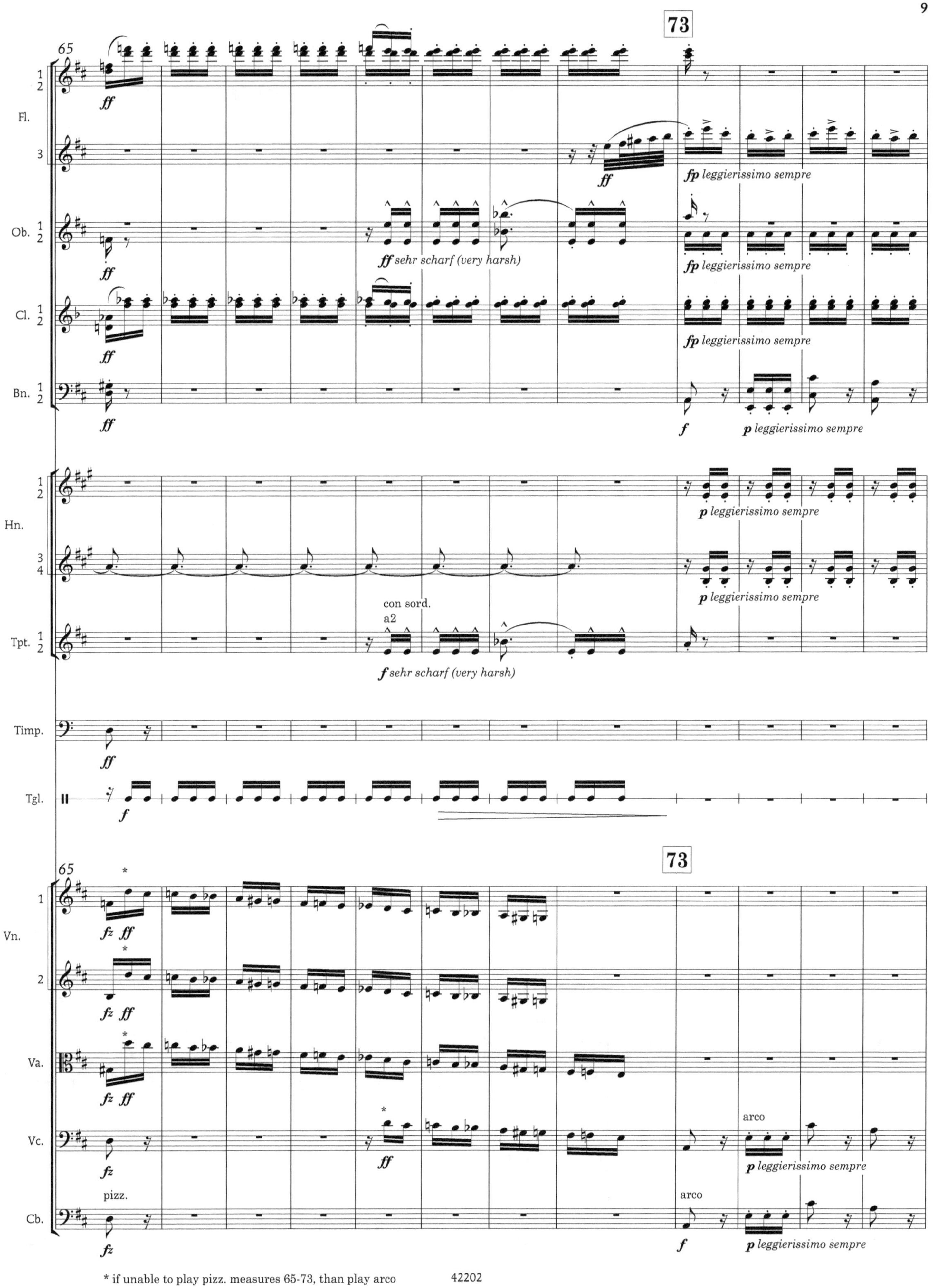

* if unable to play pizz. measures 65-73, than play arco

89
77
Fl.
1
2
3
p leggierissimo sempre
p
Ob.
Cl.
Bn.
f
Hn.
4
Tpt.
Timp.
Tgl.
Vn.
arco
Va.
Vc.
Cb.

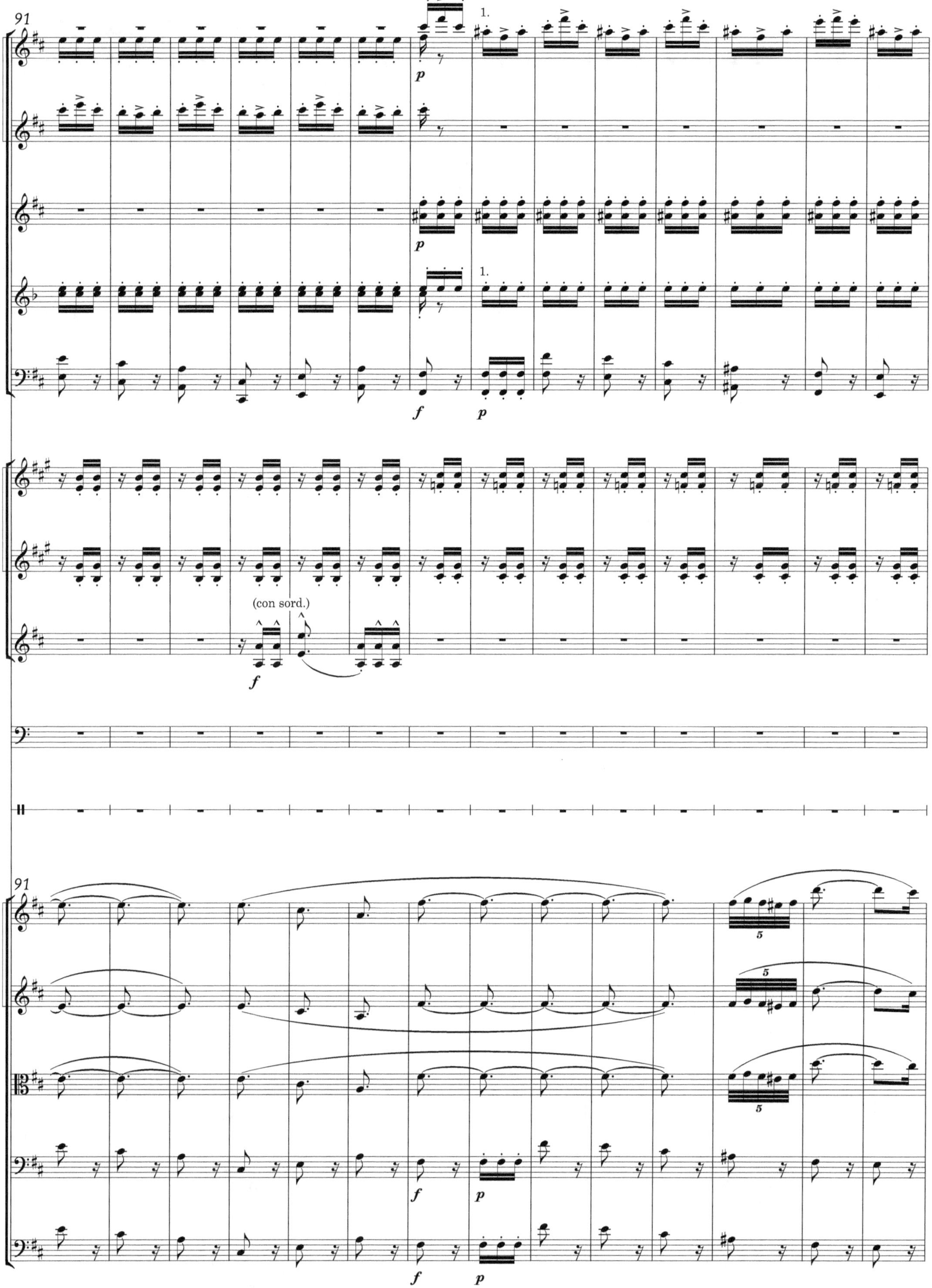

91
Fl.
Ob.
Cl.
Bn.
Hn.
Tpt.
Timp.
Tgl.
Vn.
Va.
Vc.
Cb.
(con sord.)
1.

105
Fl.
1
2
3
p
to picc.
cresc. sempre
Ob.
1.
Cl.
Bn.
f
p cresc. sempre
Hn.
3
4
Tpt.
Timp.
Tgl.
105
Vn.
Va.
Vc.
Cb.

119
121
Picc.
p cresc. sempre
ff
Fl. 1 2
ff
Ob. 1 2
ff
Cl. 1 2
ff
Bn. 1 2
ff
Hn. 1 2
ff
3 4
ff
Tpt. 1 2
a2
f cresc.
senza sord.
Timp.
Tgl.
119
121
Vn. 1
ff
2
ff
Va.
ff
Vc.
ff
Cb.
ff

So viel als möglich treiben
(push ahead as much as possible)

So viel als möglich treiben
(push ahead as much as possible)

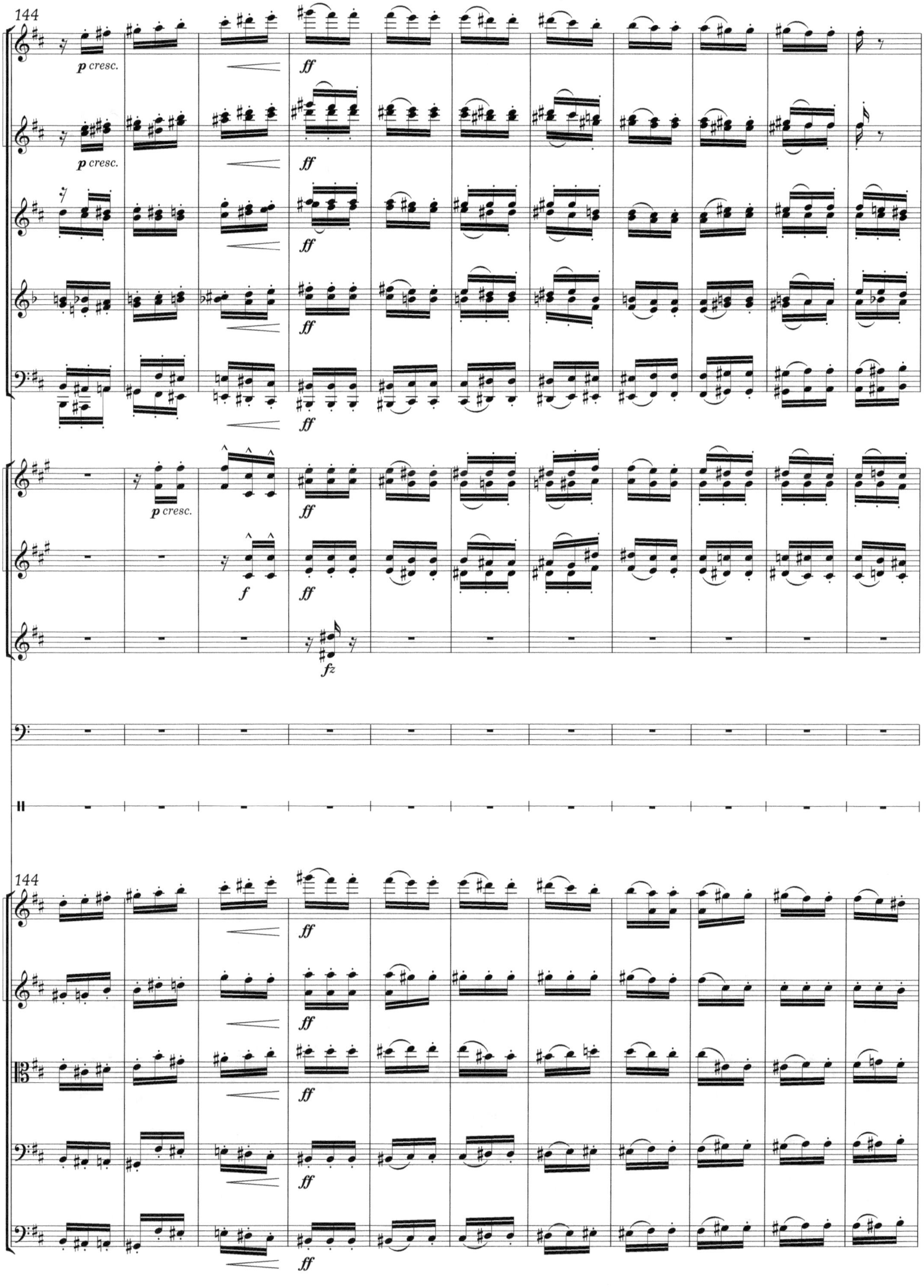
144
Picc.
p cresc.
ff
Fl. 1 2
p cresc.
ff
Ob. 1 2
ff
Cl. 1 2
ff
Bn. 1 2
ff
Hn. 1 2
p cresc.
ff
3 4
f
ff
Tpt. 1 2
fz
Timp.
Tgl.
144
Vn. 1
ff
2
ff
Va.
ff
Vc.
ff
Cb.
ff

155
159
Picc.
Fl. 1 2
Ob. 1 2
Cl. 1 2
Bn. 1 2
a2
Hn. 1 2 3 4
Tpt. 1 2
Timp.
Tgl.
Vn. 1 2
Va.
Vc.
Cb.
f
f sempre

169
Picc.
f
f
cresc.
Fl. 1 2
cresc.
Ob. 1 2
cresc.
Cl. 1 2
cresc.
Bn. 1 2
cresc.
a2
Hn. 1 2
cresc.
3 4
cresc.
Tpt. 1 2
cresc.
Timp.
f
cresc.
Tgl.
169
Vn. 1
cresc.
2
cresc.
Va.
cresc.
Vc.
Cb.

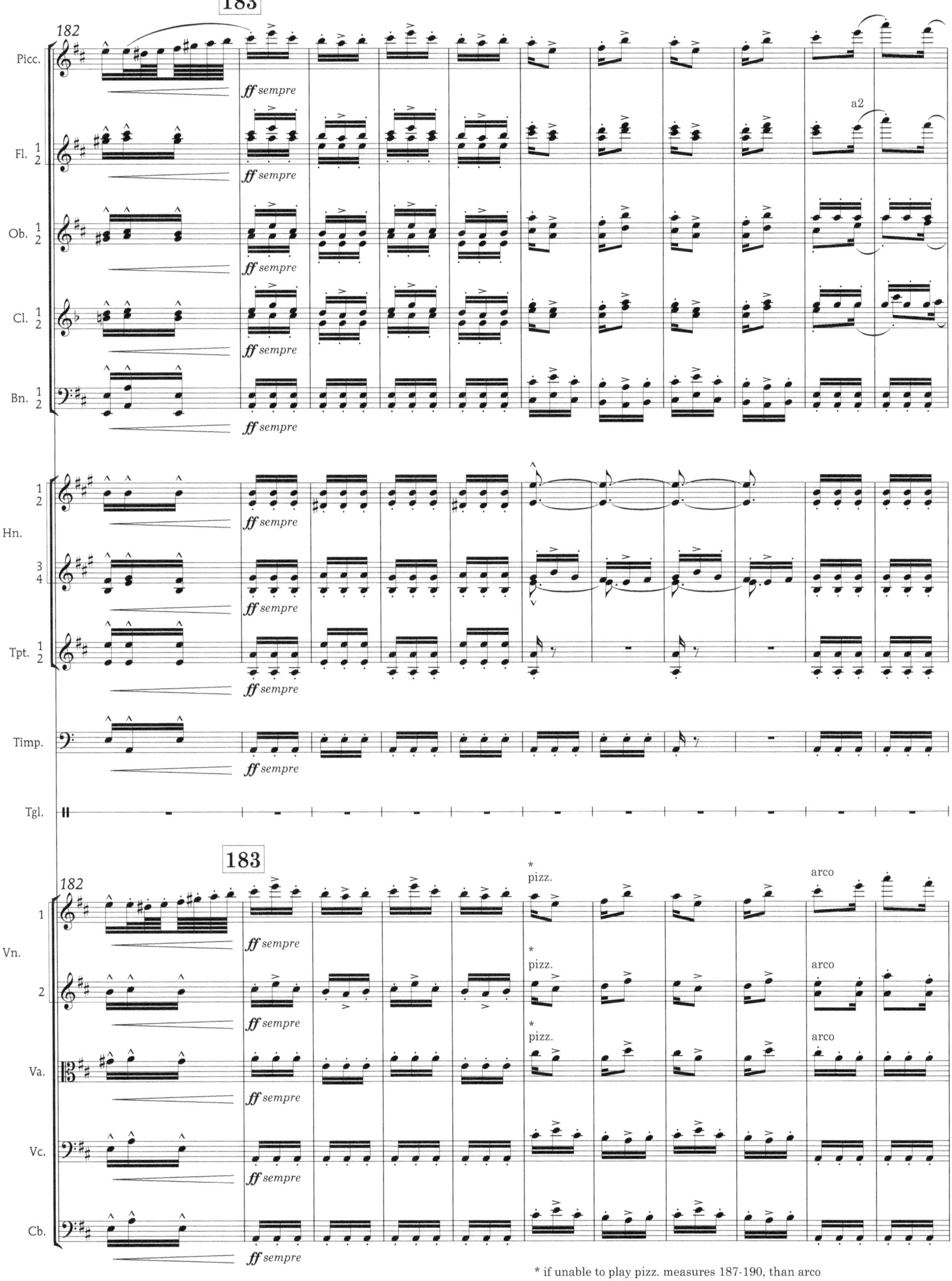

* if unable to play pizz. measures 187-190, than arco

193
199
Picc.
Fl. 1 2
Ob. 1 2
Cl. 1 2
Bn. 1 2
Hn. 1 2 3 4
Tpt. 1 2
a2
f
ff
Timp.
f
ff
Tgl.
193
199
Vn. 1 2
Va.
Vc.
Cb.

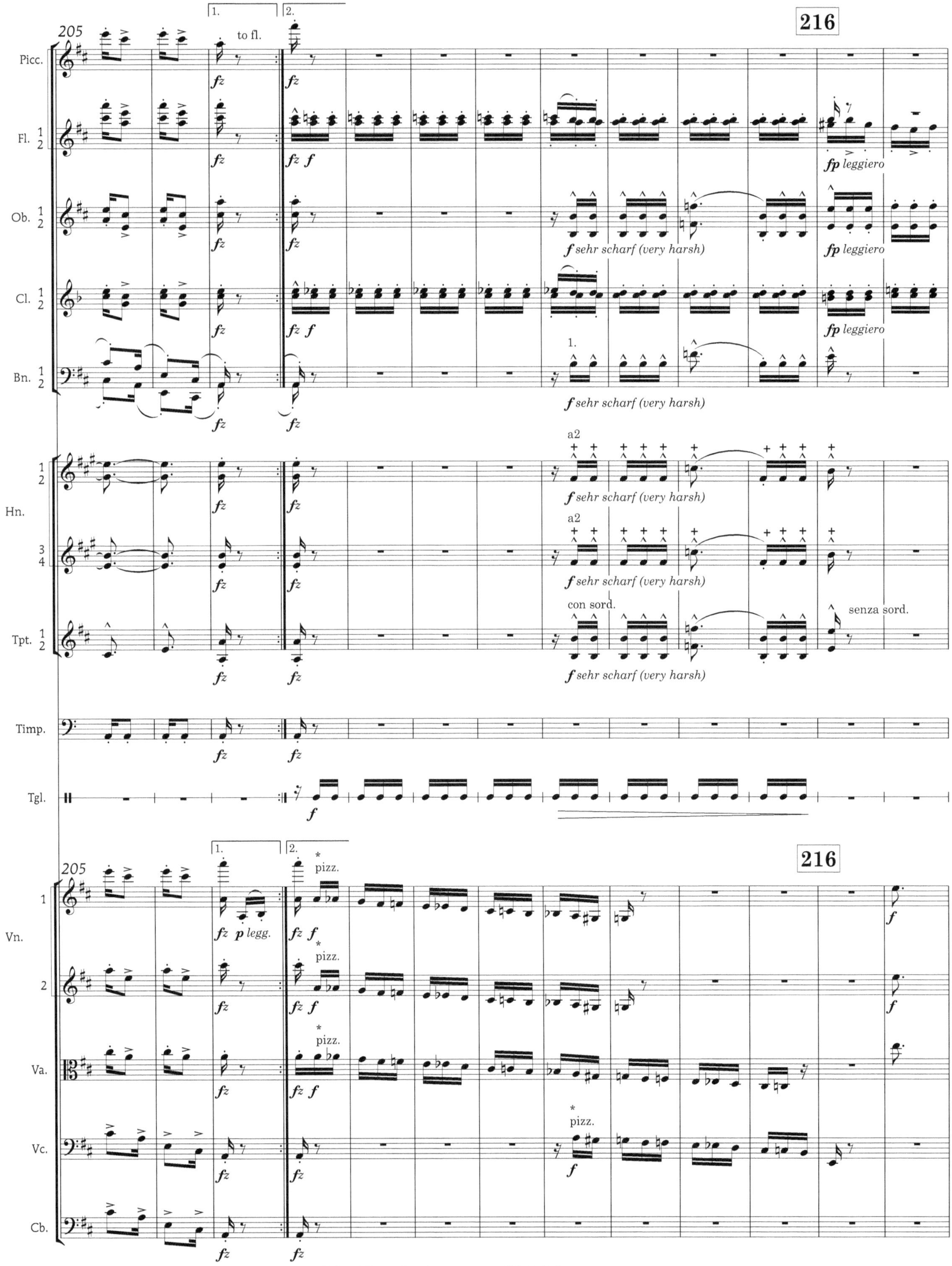

* if unable to play pizz. measures 208-216, than arco

218
Picc.
Fl. 1 2
Ob. 1 2
Cl. 1 2
Bn. 1 2
Hn. 1 2
3 4
Tpt. 1 2
Timp.
Tgl.
Vn. 1
2
Va.
Vc.
Cb.
f
p leggiero
1.
p
arco
pizz.

232
231
Picc.
ff sempre
Fl. 1 2
a2
ff sempre
Ob. 1 2
ff sempre
Cl. 1 2
ff sempre
Bn. 1 2
a2
ff sempre
Hn. 1 2
a2
ff sempre
3 4
a2
ff sempre
(senza sord.)
Tpt. 1 2
f
Timp.
f
Tgl.
232
231
Vn. 1
ff sempre
f
2
ff sempre
Va.
ff sempre
Vc.
ff sempre
Cb.
ff sempre

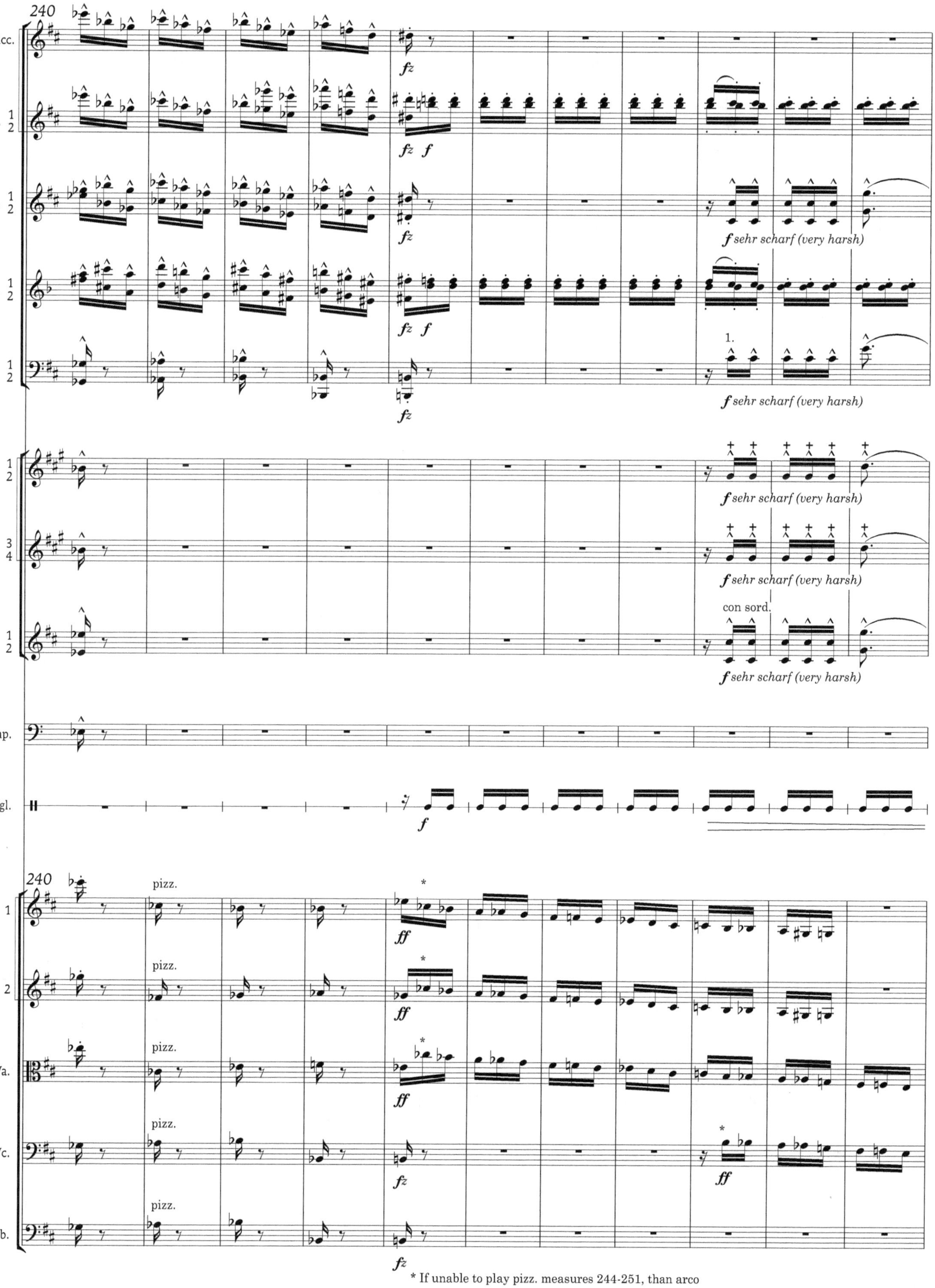

* If unable to play pizz. measures 244-251, than arco

251
252
Picc.
Fl. 1 2
Ob. 1 2
Cl. 1 2
Bn. 1 2
Hn. 1 2 3 4
Tpt. 1 2
Timp.
Tgl.
Vn. 1 2
Va.
Vc.
Cb.
fz
p leggiero
1.
to fl.
p
dim. sempre
p dim. sempre
pp
p dim.

266
268
Fl. 1 2
p con grazioso, leggiero
Ob. 1 2
p leggiero
Cl. 1 2
1.
p con grazioso,
Vn. 1 2
Va.
Vc.
arco
pp sempre
Cb.
arco
pp sempre
282
284
Ob. 1 2
1.
p molto espress.
Cl. 1 2
leggiero
Va.
p leggiero

300
Ob. 1 2
5
Cl. 1 2
300
Vn. 1
2
Va.
Vc.
Cb.
316
Ob. 1 2
1.
Cl. 1 2
f con passione
316
Vn. 1
2
Va.
Vc.
Cb.

332
Ob. 1 2
f con passione
Cl. 1 2
332
Vn. 1 2
Va.
Vc.
Cb.
348
Ob. 1 2
Cl. 1 2
348
arco
p cresc.
cresc.
arco
p cresc.
cresc.
p cresc.
Vn. 1 2
Va.
Vc.
cresc.
Cb.
cresc.

364
361
Fl.
1 2
3
p
p leggiero
1.
Ob. 1 2
1.
p poco espress.
Cl. 1 2
1.
p poco espress.
Bn. 1 2
Hn. 1 2
3 4
Tpt. 1 2
Timp.
Tgl.
364
361
Vn. 1
2
div.
p sempre leggierissimo
Va.
p sempre leggierissimo
Vc.
p sempre leggierissimo
Cb.

380
375
Fl.
Ob.
Cl.
Bn.
Hn.
Tpt.
Timp.
Tgl.
Vn.
Va.
Vc.
Cb.
poco f
p
f
f espress.
tr
1.
div. pizz.
unis.
pizz.

388
Fl.
1
2
3
più f
to picc.
1.
Ob.
1
2
più f
Cl.
1
2
poco f
più f
Bn.
1
2
a2
poco f
più f
Hn.
1
2
3
4
Tpt.
1
2
Timp.
Tgl.
388
Vn.
1
2
arco
poco f
più f
Va.
Vc.
Cb.
arco
poco f
più f

404
398
Picc.
Fl. 1 2
Ob. 1 2
Cl. 1 2
Bn. 1 2
Hn. 1 2 3 4
Tpt. 1 2
Timp.
Tgl.
Vn. 1 2
Va.
Vc.
Cb.
fp leggiero sempre
unis.
pizz.
arco
1.
3.
p
f

420
409
Picc.
Fl. 1 2
1.
Ob. 1 2
Cl. 1 2
1.
p leggiero
Bn. 1 2
f
p
Hn. 1 2
3 4
Tpt. 1 2
Timp.
Tgl.
420
409
arco
p molto espress.
Vn. 1
2
Va.
Vc.
Cb.

423
Picc.
p leggiero
Fl. 1 2
p
Ob. 1 2
p
1.
Cl. 1 2
p
1.
Bn. 1 2
f
p
Hn. 1 2
3 4
Tpt. 1 2
a2 (con sord.)
f
Timp.
Tgl.
423
Vn. 1
4
2
4
Va.
4
Vc.
f
p
Cb.
f
p

444
436
Picc.
Fl. 1 2
Ob. 1 2
Cl. 1 2
Bn. 1 2
Hn. 1 2
3 4
Tpt. 1 2
Timp.
Tgl.
Vn. 1
2
Va.
Vc.
Cb.
p cresc. sempre
cresc. sempre
1.
f
p

460
448
Picc.
p cresc. sempre
ff
Fl. 1 2
cresc. sempre
Ob. 1 2
Cl. 1 2
Bn. 1 2
Hn. 1 2
3 4
Tpt. 1 2
f cresc.
senza sord.
Timp.
Tgl.
Vn. 1
2
Va.
Vc.
Cb.

36

42202

473
Picc.
Fl. 1 2
Ob. 1 2
Cl. 1 2
Bn. 1 2
Hn. 1 2 3 4
Tpt. 1 2
Timp.
Tgl.
Vn. 1 2
Va.
Vc.
Cb.
p cresc.
cresc.
ff
f
fz

38

42202

499
Picc.
Fl. 1 2
Ob. 1 2
Cl. 1 2
Bn. 1 2
Hn. 1 2 3 4
Tpt. 1 2
Timp.
Tgl.
Vn. 1 2
Va.
Vc.
Cb.
a2
cresc.
f

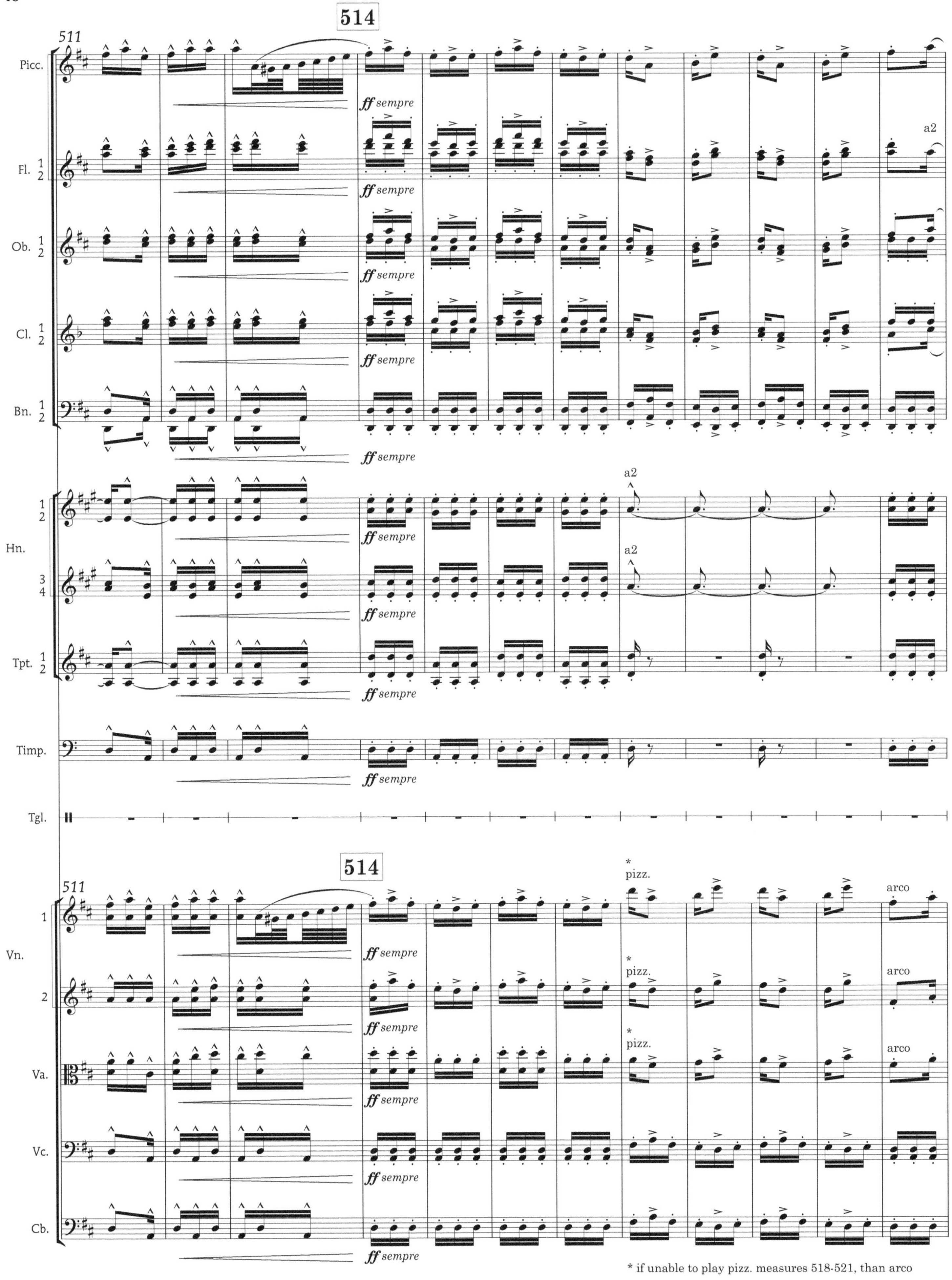

* if unable to play pizz. measures 518-521, than arco

523
530
Picc.
Fl. 1 2
Ob. 1 2
Cl. 1 2
Bn. 1 2
Hn. 1 2
3 4
Tpt. 1 2
a2
Timp.
Tgl.
Vn. 1
2
Va.
Vc.
Cb.
ff

532
Picc.
Fl. 1 2
p cresc.
Ob. 1 2
p cresc.
a2
Cl. 1 2
p cresc.
Bn. 1 2
p cresc.
Hn. 1 2
Hn. 3 4
Tpt. 1 2
Timp.
pp cresc.
Tgl.
532
Vn. 1
Vn. 2
pizz.
Va.
p cresc.
pizz.
Vc.
p cresc.
Cb.

Etwas breiter
(a little boarder)

Etwas breiter
(a little boarder)

www.ingramcontent.com/pod-product-compliance
Lightning Source LLC
LaVergne TN
LVHW081322060426

835509LV00015B/1641